BLAZERS

TOP 10
UNEXPLAINED

TOP 10 URBAN LEGENDS

by Kathryn Clay

Content Consultant:
Dr. Andrew Nichols
Director of the
American Institute of Parapsychology
Gainesville, Florida

Reading Consultant:
Barbara J. Fox
Reading Specialist
Professor Emeritus
North Carolina State University

CAPSTONE PRESS
a capstone imprint

Blazers is published by Capstone Press,
1710 Roe Crest Drive, North Mankato, Minnesota 56003.
www.capstonepub.com

Books published by Capstone Press are manufactured with paper
containing at least 10 percent post-consumer waste.

Library of Congress Cataloging-in-Publication Data
Clay, Kathryn.
   Top 10 urban legends / by Kathryn Clay.
   p. cm. — (Blazers. Top 10 Unexplained)
   Summary: "Describes various urban legends in a top-ten format"—Provided by publisher.
   Includes bibliographical references and index.
   ISBN 978-1-4296-7638-0 (library binding)
   1. Urban folklore—Juvenile literature. 2. Legends—Juvenile literature. I. Title. II. Title: Top
ten urban legends.
GR78.C53 2012
398.2091732—dc23   2011034691

Editorial Credits
Mandy Robbins, editor; Veronica Correia, designer; Eric Gohl, media researcher;
   Laura Manthe, production specialist

Photo Credits
BigStockPhoto/kaija, 25
Capstone Studio/Karon Dubke, 21 (bottom right)
Corbis/Science Faction/Chip Simons, 13
Getty Images/Time Life Pictures/Al Freni, 12
Newscom/Reuters/Courtesy of YouTube, 8; Sipa Press/Anthony Behar, 11
Shutterstock/Bruce Rolff, 4–5 (background); chungking, 9; devi, cover (background),
   4 (background), 28–29; Feng Yu, 17 (back); iodrakon, 27 (front); Jagodka, 17 (front);
   jayfish, 27 (back); kanate, 23; Karin Hildebrand Lau, 21 (back); kokitom, cover (front),
   5 (front);
   Kristin Smith, 19; Medvedev Andrey, 7; Oleg Kozlov, 15 (front); Potapov Alexander,
   19 (spiders); Robyn Mackenzie, 9 (penny); Tormod Rossavik, 15 (back); Zoom Team, 22

Printed in the United States of America in Stevens Point, Wisconsin.
102011   006404WZS12

TABLE OF CONTENTS

TRUTH OR LEGEND?

The strange stories you're about to read are often stated as fact. But are they really true? Check out the top 10 urban legends, and decide for yourself.

10

9
8
7
6
5
4
3
2
1

MEXICAN HAIRLESS

A woman is traveling in Mexico. She finds a hairless dog and takes it home. A week later, she takes the dog to the vet. She finds out her new pet is really a rat—with **rabies!**

rabies—a deadly disease people and animals can get from the bite of an infected animal

9 PENNIES FROM HEAVEN

A man looks up at a tall building and sees something falling. It's a coin that was dropped from the top floor. The coin hits the man's head, cracks his skull, and kills him instantly.

FACT The hosts of the TV show *MythBusters* tested this urban legend in 2003. They proved that a penny dropped from any height cannot crack a human skull.

ALLIGATORS
IN THE SEWER

Baby alligators are sometimes kept as pets. Legend has it that pet owners in New York City flushed their gators down the toilet. The gators survived and made the **sewer** their home. Every once in a while a gator pops out of a manhole!

FACT

In 1935 *The New York Times* reported that some boys killed an alligator in a city street. It had crawled out of the sewer.

sewer—a system that carries away liquid and solid waste

A DEADLY COMBINATION

A boy pours Pop Rocks candy into his mouth. Then he takes a drink of cola. The mixture of candy and soda causes the boy's stomach to explode.

FACT Pop Rocks are sugar crystals filled with carbon dioxide gas. The gas is released when the candy gets wet. The release of gas makes a fizzing sound.

POP ROCKS
Crackling Candy
NET WT 0.17 OZ.

POP ROCKS
Crackling Candy
NET WT 0.17 OZ.

TASTES LIKE CHICKEN

A family eats fried chicken at a fast-food restaurant. One piece is tougher than the others. When the family looks closer, they realize it is a deep-fried rat.

FACT

In 2005 a woman said she found a fingertip in her fast-food meal. It was later discovered that she put it there herself. She got the finger from a friend who had accidentally cut his finger off.

DEADLY MISTAKE

A woman gives her small dog a bath. She doesn't have much time to dry it, so she sticks it in the microwave. To her horror, the woman comes back to find the dog cooked.

FACT Never test this legend at home. Microwaving an animal would kill it!

HORRIFYING HAIRDO

A woman with a **beehive** hairdo gets quite the surprise. Hundreds of spiders crawl down her neck as she washes her hair. The spiders had made a nest in her stiff updo.

FACT As hair styles have changed, so has this urban legend. One version tells of spiders that made a nest in a man's dreadlocks.

beehive—a popular hairdo from the 1960s that resulted in a stiff shape that looked like a beehive

THE CLOWN STATUE

A babysitter is watching TV. But she is distracted by a clown statue. The sitter calls the father and asks if she can cover up the creepy statue. The father tells her to take the kids next door and call the police. The family doesn't own a clown statue.

FACT

In some versions of this story, the clown is a harmless homeless person. In other versions he is a killer.

A RUDE AWAKENING

A man wakes up in a hotel bathtub full of ice. His side is aching. He looks down and sees stitches. Someone removed his kidney in the middle of the night!

THE DISAPPEARING HITCHHIKER

A man is driving at night and sees a **hitchhiker**. He offers the young woman a ride. She accepts and gives the driver her address. When they reach her house, the woman has mysteriously disappeared.

hitchhiker–a person who travels by getting rides from strangers

The driver rings the doorbell, and an old man answers. The driver explains what happened. He learns that the hitchhiker was the old man's daughter. She died in a car crash many years earlier.

FACT

Many versions of this story exist. In one version, the hitchhiker borrows the driver's sweater. The driver finds it in a nearby cemetery.

UNBELIEVABLE!

Sometimes urban legends are made up as warnings. Other urban legends start out with some truth but are **exaggerated**. Either way, it's fun to retell mysterious urban legends.

exaggerate–to make something seem bigger, better, or more important than it actually is

Glossary

beehive (BEE-hyv)—a popular hairdo from the 1960s that resulted in a stiff shape that looked like a beehive

exaggerate (eg-ZAJ-uh-rate)—to make something seem bigger, better, or more important than it actually is

hitchhiker (HICH-hy-kuhr)—a person who travels by getting rides from strangers

kidney (KID-nee)—an organ that filters waste products from the blood and turns them into urine

rabies (RAY-beez)—a deadly disease people and animals can get from the bite of an infected animal

sewer (SOO-ur)—a system that carries away liquid and solid waste

urban legend (ER-buhn LEH-jund)—an odd or unlikely story that is often told as if it were true

Read More

Lynette, Rachel. *Urban Legends.* Mysterious Encounters. Detroit: KidHaven Press, 2008.

O'Shei, Tim. *Creepy Urban Legends.* Scary Stories. Mankato, Minn.: Capstone Press, 2011.

Regan, Lisa, and Chris McNab. *Urban Myths and Legendary Creatures.* Monsters & Myths. New York: Gareth Stevens Pub., 2011.

Internet Sites

FactHound offers a safe, fun way to find Internet sites related to this book. All of the sites on FactHound have been researched by our staff.

Here's all you do:

Visit *www.facthound.com*

Type in this code: 9781429676380

Super-cool stuff!

Check out projects, games and lots more at
www.capstonekids.com

Index